YOUR KNOWLEDGE HAS VALUE

Bibliographic information published by the German National Library:

The German National Library lists this publication in the National Bibliography; detailed bibliographic data are available on the Internet at http://dnb.dnb.de .

Imprint:

Copyright © 2007 GRIN Verlag, Open Publishing GmbH
Print and binding: Books on Demand GmbH, Norderstedt Germany
ISBN: 9783640676897

This book at GRIN:

http://www.grin.com/en/e-book/154729/rio-bravo-the-antidote-to-high-noon

Birgit Wilpers

'Rio Bravo' - The antidote to 'High Noon'?

GRIN Publishing

GRIN - Your knowledge has value

Since its foundation in 1998, GRIN has specialized in publishing academic texts by students, college teachers and other academics as e-book and printed book. The website www.grin.com is an ideal platform for presenting term papers, final papers, scientific essays, dissertations and specialist books.

Visit us on the internet:

http://www.grin.com/

http://www.facebook.com/grincom

http://www.twitter.com/grin_com

Universität Paderborn

Fakultät für Kulturwissenschaften
Institut für Anglistik und Amerikanistik
Sommersemester 2007
Proseminar: How the West was won

Term Paper:

Rio Bravo – the antidote to *High Noon*?

Birgit Wilpers

1. Introduction

„Rio Bravo was made because I didn't like a picture called *High Noon*" (McBride 130). This is one of Howard Hawks' comments on his movie *Rio Bravo*, which he directed and produced in 1959. In this essay, I will describe the main features of Rio Bravo, deliver a possible interpretation of the characters and finally point out some of the main differences and similarities between *Rio Bravo* and *High Noon*.

2. Setting

The film is set in a little village in Texas. All scenes take place in only very few locations: the main street, the jail, the hotel, one of the saloons and at the outskirts of the village (Burdette's warehouse) during the showdown. "'Hawks' town consists of jail, hotel, saloons, and rows of inconspicuous house-fronts [...]" (Lusted 161). The main street shows a few shops and business fronts, only leading to several houses of Mexican inhabitants at the end of the town, behind them the desert begins.

The motif of landscape and creation of space – contrary to many other westerns, for instance, directed by John Ford – lacks completely. "[F]or Hawks the West is simply the stage on which his characters [...] move. Accordingly, there is no feel of the West in *Rio Bravo*" (Hardy 269). Nevertheless, an atmosphere of threat is created, though not from the surrounding wilderness, but instead of from the powerful villain, Nathan Burdette, and his followers.

3. The plot – a short summary

The plot can be divided into four parts that is to say the events take place during the course of four days and nights. John T. Chance, the sheriff of a small village in Texas, arrests Joe Burdette because he killed a man in the saloon. He puts him in jail and has to wait for six days until the marshall will arrive in the town and take Joe with him. During these six days Burdette's brother Nathan, a rich farmer, tries to liberate Joe out of the jail by all means and "bottles up the town" (all quotations are transcribed from the movie). He hires paid killers and makes them shoot a friend of Chance, who had wanted to help him. The Sheriff and his group have to deal with several attacks, until, eventually, it comes to the final showdown at Burdette's warehouse, where an exchange between Joe and Dude, the deputy sheriff, whom the Burdettes kept as a hostage, should take place. The sheriff defeats the gang together with his group.On the fourth day, this final showdown takes place and the day ends with a humorous scene again in the evening, when Feathers makes Chance declare her his love – a happy ending, of course.

This plot can be called a professional plot: there is a heterogeneous group of heroes which form a team together. Each of them has certain characteristics or special skills and they have to come to an arrangement together in order to fullfil a mission. Usually, the group fights for a weak community, but in the case of *Rio Bravo*, the community is not set in the foreground. Instead of that, the members of the group have different motives to fight, for example, in order to regain self-respect (Dude).

> […] the essential qualification is to work together […]. This also means that members of the group also have human failings. Acknowledging this, the hero invariably asks only if those who join the group are 'good enough' (Lusted 161-162).

A question repeatedly asked by the sheriff during the movie. Chance: "Think you're good enough?" Dude: "I'd like to find out." Chance: "So would I".

4. Characterization

4.1 John T. Chance (John Wayne)

It is made clear to the audience that the sheriff is the hero of *Rio Bravo*. He also functions as a father figure to his companions. He helps them to overcome their personal failures (Dean Martin as the drunk), he takes care for them and tries to protect them from any harm, even endangering his own life, and he is the independent, strong and competent male figure. In short, he knows what is right and wrong and has no problems in sticking consequently to his principles. Wheeler, his friend, refers to Chance as a person who is surely "holding a bull by the tail.", when he refuses to accept help from him. This is one of the main topics of the movie: the refusal to accept support from others.

Chance's role as a father figure is obvious from many dialogues thoughout the movie, especially when dealing with Dude, who at one point ironically answers him "Yes, Papa". The sheriff does not only have a strong physical presence through the outward appearance of John Wayne, the Western hero par excellence, but he needs psychological qualities as well in order to succeed in the forthcoming conflict and to hold his 'family' together.

Hence, the figure of John T. Chance always remains a little bit isolated from the other characters, first of all, because he is the boss, but also because he refuses to accept help from his friends, although he desperately needs it, facing the overwhelming power of his enemies. For example, he does not join in the joyful singing of his deputies in one scene, instead of that he watches it with mild amusement.

4.2 Dude (Dean Martin)

Dude is the wrecked alcoholic, the lost son, the man without self-respect on account of an unhappy love-affair. Already during the first scene in the saloon, the viewer is made aware of the father-son relation between Chance and him, when Chance helps him, while Dude is humiliated by the villain, Joe Burdette. There is no dialogue at all during this scene and there is no need to, as everything is made clear by acting and appearance: Dude's worn-out clothes, the shaking of his hands, his eager look at Burdette's glass of whiskey. The development of Dude from the hopeless drunkard to a recovered and respectable member of society again is also one of the main topics of the movie. The sheriff seems to be the only person who still believes in Dude's abilities, as he has kept his guns and his clothes for him: "Been waiting till they fit you again" (Chance). Dude has to undergo several trials of reliability, for example, in Burdette's saloon, where people make fun of him: "Dude, you've been seeing things again. You better have a drink". Initially, he passes these tests, until we come to one of the key scenes of the movie, when he begins to doubt in his abilities once again, since the Burdette gang overwhelmed him at his guard. He wants to quit the 'family' and Chance leaves the decision up to him, even saying: "He can take the whole bottle". Eventually, Dude goes through a moment of catharsis and self-recognition, when he hears the tune of "The Deguello" and finally wants to quit drinking himself. The "cutthroat song", which was played by "the Mexicans for the Texas boys when they had them bottled up at the Alamo" (Colorado), is a symbol for the approaching fight the group is awaiting. Their enemy, Nathan Burdette, instructed the Mexican band to play it the whole day in order to threaten the group.

4.3 Stumpy (Walter Brennan)

He is the hero's sidekick and he functions as a comic relief as well, which is the same role as he had in Red River (1948, Howard Hawks). In Hawks' words: "I've seen so many people laugh at violence when it happens. [...] So I start out and try to get their attention with a good dramatic sequence, and then find a place to start getting some laughs" (McBride 66-67). One example is the dramatic scene, already mentioned, when Dude finally decides to quit drinking and Stumpy's comment is: "Nobody ever asks me if I need a drink. […] You two are enough to drive a man to it". Walter Brennan plays the part of the grumpy old man, who – on the other hand – takes lovable care for his peer group, not only in the literal sense that he cooks for them and provides them with coffee, beer and tobacco, but also at a crucial point of the showdown, when he participates in it and has the idea to use dynamite, which eventually leads to their victory.

4.4 Feathers (Angie Dickinson)

Feathers is the only appearance of a female character in *Rio Bravo*, apart from the Mexican Consuela, the wife of the hotel owner Carlos. Feathers is an independent woman, she travels around the country earning her own money by gambling, which is not a very respectable way for a woman to make her living, considering the moral principles of the American West in the 19th century. From the very beginning she makes it clear that she is romantically interested in Chance by provoking him and even embarrassing him, for instance, telling him to search her in order to prove that she was the card-sharper. Feather is a mixture between the respectable woman and the bad girl, two of the typical stereotypes of the Western. Initially, the viewer may think that she is the bad girl, since Chance confronts her with a handbill searching for her and an accomplice. During a later dialogue between the two of them, though, it becomes clear that she is basically a good woman, as she answers Chance's question how a girl gets herself on a handbill with the explanation:"She gets married". Besides, the viewer also learns that Chance's past is probably neither very respectable, since he answers the question how he became Sherrif with:"He gets tired of selling his gun all over. Decides to sell it in one place", which is an allusion that he might have been a gunman. In the course of the plot, Feathers becomes more and more the respectable woman, as she supports and tries to protect the Sheriff.

4.5 Colorado (Ricky Nelson)

He plays the young gunman who is at first indifferent towards the sheriff's problems and does not want to help him. Nevertheless, he changes his attitude when his boss Wheeler is killed by the villains and joins the group. However, throughout the whole story he remains a bland character. "Hawks gets him to do as little as possible and to stand as far back in the frame as the narrative and his contract permit" (Mast 359). The reasons for his appearance in the movie might have been of commercial nature, since he was a very popular singer during the Fifties.

As Howard Hawks commented: "And we got a million dollars more than we usually did [with Ricky Nelson], so I thought that worked out pretty well" (McBride 126).

4.6 The Mexicans

In *Rio Bravo* the Mexicans are depicted as a stereotype. They live on the fringe of the village in typical Mexican-style houses. They work for the Americans, take care for the horses or, as shown in one scene, lie drunk on a bench. The Mexican couple, Carlos and Consuela, who own the hotel, are loyal to the Sheriff and described as kind and honest people, but simultaneously they are characterized by a sympathetic dullness and submission to the sheriff. Chance gives orders to Carlos which he immediately follows. In addition, the role of Carlos has the function of a comic relief as well. He is under the thumb of his wife, he misunderstands instructions due to his broken English and he is not even capable of handling a gun during the showdown – one of the basic capacities a 'real' man in a Western should have. Hence, the Mexicans figures of the movie remain inferior to the white characters.

5. The role of the woman

Feathers is the forcing power behind the development of the romance between her and the sheriff. Chance does not know how to deal with her as she is independent, self-confident and even slightly sexually provoking: "You will have to search me". Indeed, even his friends have to give him advise how to deal with her. During the course of the movie, she becomes a supporter of the Sheriff and his male family, but, certainly, only in the sense of a 'weak woman', for instance, throwing flower pots through windows to distract the villains. As a matter of fact, she could never become a real member of the male family for the simple reason that she is a woman. Concerning personal interactions between men and women, she seems to be much more experienced than the Sheriff, though. Hawks himself says about the role of the women in his movies: "I've been accused of promoting Women's Lib, and I've denied it, emphatically. […] I'd reverse it and let the girl do the chasing around" (McBride 96). Indeed, the women are the forcing power concerning romance, but they still remain only supportive characters to the male heroic actions. This is "the illusion of autonomy […] less a sign of maturity than an imitation of the male, the highest form of flattery. Hawks's characters exist in pre-social or tribal situations dominated by the male group. Women are defind in relation to its style and values" (Kitses 30).

6

6. The community versus the family

In *Rio Bravo* the community remains in the background, unlike many other classical Westerns. Although the sheriff and his deputies are members of the community and representatives of them, they are simultaneously outsiders: the past of Chance is ambiguous, Stumpy is a "cripple", Dude is a notorious drunk and Colorado is a teenage gunman, who comes from another city. Their supporters are neither depicted as community members: Feathers is a stranger and the Mexican couple belongs to another ethnic group. On the contrary, there are the Burdettes, rich farmers, who probably achieved their wealth by stealing it from the honest, small farmers. In one scene in the jail it is indicated that Burdette took away land from Stumpy. Inside this structure, the community of the village remains rather abstract, like an unknown mass. They only appear on the scene, when there is a chance to watch a gunfight, for example, when the exchange of Dude and Joe Burdette is going to take place.

The emphasis of the movie is laid on the interpersonal relations of the group around the sheriff and their interactions. In this sense, one could call the movie a chamberplay, a drama, which just happens to take place in the Wild West, but which could be transferred into any other setting. *Rio Bravo* is principally dealing with the formation of a male 'family', who have to fulfill a task together; it tells a story about male camaraderie and friendship. "The group acts not just for the good of the wider community but because they judge it justifies their own collectivity" (Lusted 161). Their credo is absolute loyality and support to each other, responsibility for and identification with the group in order to fullfil their adapted task. Despite of the fact that Chance always refuses to accept help and even forbids Stumpy to participate in the exchange of Dude and Burdette, he obtains assistance from all sides and especially during the showdown from Stumpy. This showdown scene clearly points out that the group has grown together as a 'family', even though they have remained individuals throughout the story line with different personal problems, for instance, Dude's drinking problem and with different motivations for their doings. However, they were able to overcome personal difficulties with the support of the various group members and work together as a team for the fulfillment of their common objective.

7. A comparison to High Noon

The setting of *Rio Bravo* is similar to Fred Zinnemann's *High Noon* (1952), where the story also takes place in a little town. However, Zinnemann's Hadleyville seems to be much more civilized, since the viewer can see a thriving community, with churches, several shops, people promenading around the town, which even has a railway station – the gateway to civilization.

In both movies we have a main hero – the sheriff of the town, whereby Gary Cooper in *High Noon* is a well-respected, even domesticated member of the community. One of the introductory scenes is his marriage scene with all his friends as guests. The main difference between both heros is their behaviour. Cooper asks desperately for support in his fight against the villains, but he does not get it – not even from his supposed best friends. Eventually, he has to combat the villains all alone and only his wife helps him. In Hawks' words: "I didn't think a good Sheriff was going to go running around town like a chicken with his head off asking for help, and finally his Quaker wife had to save him. That isn't my idea of a good Western Sheriff." (McBride 130).

On the contrary, Hawks' Sheriff refuses to accept help, although he needs support as badly as Gary Cooper in *High Noon*. He wants to protect his friends who offer help to him from being shot. He regards them as "well-meaning amateurs" and expects that "A lot of people would get hurt", which he does not want. Eventually, especially during the showdown, it is made clear that he could not have won the fight without the full support of his group and his slight isolation from them goes up in smoke verbatim. Whereas in *High Noon* the hero fights for his community and has to realise that the silent majority has no backbone, the opposite takes place in *Rio Bravo*. The hero gets support from all sides – mainly strangers, but not necessarily from the community, the village respectively, although he keeps on refusing to accept their support.

Furthermore, the plot of both films can be discriminated against each other. Whereas in *High Noon*, the action on screen takes place in real time, a new, unusual technique to increase the suspense, and has its climax in the showdown at the end, the events in *Rio Bravo* follow a chronological order taking place during four days and nights, whereby the group has to handle several attacks of the villains.

The role of the women can also be differentiated against each other. In *High Noon*, there are two typical role models for women in Westerns: on the one hand, the good girl and respectable wife (Grace Kelly) and on the other hand the non-respectable, but good-hearted, Mexican prostitute. They are two stereotypes and build a counterpart in the movie, although both love the same man. In accordance with the moral principles of the Fifties, the hero married the blonde good girl and not the independent, black-haired woman with an ambiguous past from another ethnic group. *Rio Bravo's* main female figure is Feathers, also an independent woman who makes her own living. She is the forcing power in the romantic relationship with Chance. She has a dark past as well, which does not mean, though, that she is inacceptable for the hero.

In comparison, *High Noon* and *Rio Bravo* both play with stereotypical characters. The main difference is the behaviour of the hero and the emphasis that *Rio Bravo* lays on the professional group.

8. Conclusion

Often, *High Noon* has been regarded as a statement against the McCarthyism and "as an attack on America's growing silent majority" (Hardy 215) of the Fifties. However, against the political background of the Cold War, one could also interpret it as the exact opposite: the failure of America to fight against the threat of communism. "It is said that after [...] Zinnemann's putatively anti-McCarthy *High Noon* appeared, Howard Hawks made *Rio Bravo* as a rebuttal, but most previewers perceived both movies simply as expressions of the heroism in the peace officers' professionalism" (Cripps 175).

Rio Bravo, may be interpreted as the antidote to *High Noon*, stating that a strong hero (or country) does not need any help, but he (it) will nevertheless find the necessary support, as long as he presents himself strong enough and fights for the right values – honor, integrity and self-respect.

References

Hawks, Howard, dir./prod. *Rio Bravo*. Perf. John Wayne, Dean Martin, Ricky Nelson, Angie Dickinson, Walter Brennan. Armada Productions, 1959. DVD, renewed Warner Home Video, 2001.

Bibliography

Cripps, Thomas. *Hollywood's High Noon*. Baltimore: John Hopkins University Press, 1997.

Hardy, Phil. *The Western*. London: Aurum Press, 1983.

Kitses, Jim. *Horizons West. New Edition*. London: British Film Institute, 2004.

Lusted, David. *The western*. Harlow: Longman, 2003.

Mast, Gerald. *Howard Hawks, Storyteller*. New York: Oxford University Press, 1982.

McBride, Joseph. *Hawks on Hawks*. Berkeley: University of California Press, 1982.